Acknowledgement

To those that brave the heat of the flame, the depth of the rapidly flowing water and the dangers of flowing mud to save others, including our beloved pets,
I salute you for your bravery and selflessness.

I can't forget Ruth, who keeps me straight when my mind starts running.

Table of Contents

Introduction

I have been an emergency, evacuation, volunteer coordinator and manager for more than 5 years for large animals. During my volunteer evacuations, I have been stepped on, spit on, slobbered on, kicked, butted, dragged and slammed against plenty of walls. I have also been a shoulder to cry on, a Zen Master to calm owners, and a ring leader when the animals go everywhere except where they are supposed to go. I have been presenting the Plan, Prepare, and Implement Clinics since 2014. My PPI clinics range from the classroom PowerPoint presentations to animal participation in arenas. There is a combination of important details with life-saving humor, and together this has led to the clinic and evacuation successes and referrals. After years of personally seeing how quickly events can turn tragic because of the lack of preparedness, I decided to offer my clinics on a broader scale and to work towards providing large animal owners with additional tools that will help them to better handle emergency situations involving their animals.

Plan, Prepare and Implement Evacuation Training was originally created as an audience presentation format, although it is really much more interactive and entertaining. Due to many requests, I've developed this handbook to use as a guideline for large animal emergency evacuation planning for those audiences who cannot attend clinics, want to present their own clinics, or use this information as a follow up to a clinic they attended.

PPI will guide you through the steps necessary to successfully evacuate your animals before they or you are put in danger. It will help you plan in advance, determine when to prepare and what to do, and indicate how to handle the evacuation process when you need to evacuate.

While reading this book, you will find that many of the examples not only apply to emergency evacuations but also to day-to-day emergency events. By following this plan, you will see how preparing for a natural disaster will help whether you're at a horse show, at a fair, on the highway or out on the trail.

Chapter I

Plan......

What Is In A Plan?

The key to any successful event is to plan. Planning is necessary for taking a vacation, creating a family, buying a house and properly handling an emergency or natural disaster. Please note, I say "taking a vacation" first. I cannot lie. To me, vacation planning is the best kind of planning to do, especially when you take your horses with you. The most important type of planning you could do is to prepare for an emergency, whether it is an accident in the show ring or driving on the highway or riding on the trail. Emergencies usually come unannounced and often in natural disaster form, as many of you have learned. How you handle these emergencies will decide if the outcome is tragic or has a safe and happy ending. Proper planning will help ensure the outcome is the safe, happy ending.

Planning does not only mean to prepare for yourself. This applies to your family, friends and animals. All should be involved in the emergency planning process. The key to successful planning is communication. The more your friends, family and animals are prepared, the more cohesive and calm the emergency will be handled. Ah, yes, that thing called "communication." Many think "communication" is something that needs speech and direct interaction. It is amazing how many people think they are not communicating just because they are not talking. Has anyone ever tried standing calmly while someone walks up to them and suddenly starts jumping around like a madwoman? The person standing still will either run as fast as she can or call the police to report a crazy lady. The person approaching and jumping around has communicated and did not even have to say anything. We may not be able to talk to our animals (I do, but I am one of those madwomen), but we can communicate with them. By planning in advance and improving our communication skills, we prepare ourselves, our family, our friends and our animals for these emergencies.

The time to start planning is NOW. You may not need to implement the following steps for the next year or two, but, by planning and reviewing your plan, you'll be ready and calm when the emergency does occur. Once you have read and understood the PPI in this handbook for changing your life, start filling out those checklists, packing your trailers and planning escape routes. Start now, not later. The longer you wait, the less likely you will be able to get the planning steps done. If you read this and don't do anything, although I will get to keep the money you spent for this handbook, you will not have benefitted. My goal is to help you plan so as to ensure that the outcome for you and your animals is safe when emergencies do occur.

Large animal evacuations and emergencies requiring transport take more energy and training since there is more involved than waking someone up or putting the cat or dog in your car and driving away. You need to train large animals to load in a trailer, mentally train them for panicked situations, prepare them to be handled by others, and also train them to handle unfamiliar, often chaotic, environments. Therefore, it is important to start planning Now. I can't emphasize Now enough. Part of planning for large animal emergencies is helping them learn your communication. Ah, yes, that "communication" thing again. They need to learn how important it is to load quickly into a trailer, yours or another's, and you will only be able to teach this by communication.

There are multiple aspects of planning: Planning your emergency contacts, planning routes, planning supplies, planning emergency needs, planning your trailer set up and more. The first step is your emergency contact list. This applies to large animal communities, boarding facilities, and HOA's.

Who Can you Trust

Who can you trust when it comes to handling your large animals? When I say, "who can you trust", I don't mean your future spouse, the masked man at the grocery store or the vacuum salesman at your front door. I am referring to identification of the people that you trust to handle and make decisions for your large animals if you are not available. You need to find people you can rely on to care for your large animals, take them to safety and make good decisions on their behalf. Not an easy task. At clinics I used to refer to the audience's partners as one of the people that could be relied upon. All too often I got a look of horror when I said this. So, I asked, "you don't trust your spouse or significant other?" The normal response was that they did trust each other but there was no way they trusted their partner with their horse, llama, goat, or even their Brahma bull. There it is, they trusted their partner to go to Hawaii with a model but not with their large animal. I am always glad that we "communicated" this. There is a method for figuring out who you can trust with your large animals. This method requires consistent communication, time and *planning*. The first reason to start planning now is because you may think your best riding partner is someone you can trust until you realize they feed their animal beer to calm him down. You'll need to find someone else to trust.

The goal for planning is to find not just one person to trust but two or three or four. Hopefully, you know that many trustworthy people. You can always borrow friends of friends. Once you've identified those people, they become your emergency contacts; and they should vary by geographic area and experience. Two should be within proximity of your animals but should be from opposite directions. As an example, one lives about 3 miles to the south and the other lives 5 miles to the north. By having friends in different directions, you increase the ability to get your animals evacuated since emergencies usually come from different directions. Fires burn from one direction to another; mudslides usually occur in weak areas of a mountainside; and flooding comes from above and below. The third contact should be someone a little farther away who is outside your immediate zone. If nothing else, this person can help communicate with the others. However, they may also be your only source if the other two emergency contacts are affected by the same emergency as you or are otherwise unavailable.

If you are at a boarding facility, I recommend you find five people that you can trust. Two or three of those people should have trailers. If you have a trailer yourself, find people who may need help evacuating their animals. Additionally, you will want to name one person who does not keep their animal at the same place and make sure they are identified as authorized handlers on your boarding agreement.

Once you have named your emergency contacts, it is time to socialize. Yes, it is okay to read that sentence again as it may sound strange that I recommend socializing in an emergency planning handbook. Have a BBQ, get your community together, and get approval for a BBQ at your boarding facility. Great food and beverages can bring different people together for a mutually beneficial purpose to:

- Plan the emergency exits

- Plan meeting destinations

- Identify comfort levels of handling your animals and maybe your truck and trailer

- Get availability schedules of those who are becoming your emergency contacts

- Show your contacts where you keep spare keys (truck and trailers), emergency halters, supplies and ownership portfolio (we'll get to that later)

- Show your contacts how to operate your equipment. Suggestion, if your social event involves alcohol, I highly recommend you do this prior to drinking anything

- Complete the Emergency Contact forms

Emergency Contact forms are important documents for you and your emergency contact people. They give all the information for your animals, hidden key locations, and an opportunity to identify any behavioral problems or health issues of your animal. Also, they identify emergency evacuation sites by order of availability, and they can be used as a consent form if you have to take them to an emergency evacuation site or need medical treatment. Together, walk the grounds with your contact people and show everyone where the gear, supplies and emergency keys are located.

This form also has one more piece of critical information that many do not think about - it shows the order of animals to be evacuated. I truly hope you never have to make that choice as it is heartbreaking to decide who is more important. Many people have more animals than they can haul, thus requiring some to be left behind until additional help can be found. During an emergency there is not much time, and every indecision delays evacuating. By planning and identifying the order of evacuees, your decision has been made, and you are mentally prepared. I hope you find that great friend who has extra room in their trailer to take your animals if all of yours do not fit in your personal trailer. Planning ahead minimizes the chance this will happen; but if it does, it will minimize the time you or your emergency contact will take deciding who to load first.

Next page is your Neighborhood Planning worksheet. Make at least four copies of the completed form. Two should go in your Ownership Portfolio, one to keep and one to give to the evacuation site; and one should be kept in your trailer, and one goes with your evacuation friend. Don't forget your phone. Create an "Animal Evacuation Contact List" or take a picture of the completed form to keep on your phone. Also, upload this onto a shared, remote drive in case you need to access from a remote location.

You should meet with your emergency contacts about every 3 months to confirm availability, identify new emergency contacts, and discuss any changes. Remember that with good food and fun these social events become easy, and good food will almost always encourage attendance.

Neighborhood Planning worksheet

Owner(s) :

Address:

Telephone # 1   **Telephone # 2**

Closest Cross streets

# of Horses   Names, colors and breed:

# of other livestock

Trailers   *Holds how many:*

           Size

           G/N or Bumper

Other trailering options

Evacuation Order of Priority

	Name	Type
1		
2		
3		
4		
5		
6		

Trailer key Location

Truck key Location:

Meeting Locations: Parking Lots/cross streets

Evacuation site # 1

     Name

     Address

Evacuation site # 2

     Name

     Address

Authorized Contact #1

     Name:

     Telephone #

Authorized Contact #2

     Name:

     Telephone #

Authorized Contact #3

     Name:

     Telephone #

Additional: (including intake and treatment authorization)

I, _____ *authorize above contacts to make decisions for above identified animals on my behalf if I am not present.*

Owner Signature:

Keeping Your Trailer Ready

Maintaining your trailer should be something you do on a regular basis. Many people who have livestock trailers use them just enough to go locally, but one day realize they need to do a maintenance check up while they are on their way somewhere. I think one of the reasons we (I say "we" because I'm just as guilty) do this is because we can't see what it is that needs to be maintained and repaired. Unlike cars and trucks, we don't have a "service and mileage due date" sticker on the windshield staring at us every time we get in the car. Usually, we know that we need to service the trailer when something breaks or just doesn't work quite right. Very often I hear stories about horses stepping through floors, brakes giving out, faulty wires/lights and more. All these things could have been prevented by a yearly checkup. Now that I've scared you into thinking your horse or Brahma bull is going to fall out of the trailer next time you go somewhere, let's talk about keeping the trailer ready for emergencies.

Trailer maintenance should be done at least once a year. Everything I suggest going forward in this chapter is directed toward emergency planning, but it is something you should do even if you think you will never ever have any emergencies. Remember, emergencies are not just natural disasters. Emergencies happen in the middle of the night when your animal needs to go to the veterinarian; they happen when we crash on the trail; and they happen when a friend or stranger needs your help getting their animal out of a dangerous situation. Be prepared for the emergency, don't be a part of it.

The attached Trailer Maintenance Checklist highlights not only inspection points but also shows the condition of each point and what urgently needs repairing. I had to look at my own situation when I developed this format. There are plenty of great trailer safety checklists out there. From a personal aspect, I spend a lot (A LOT) of money trailering my horse, buying equipment I don't need, and buying overpriced supplements that my horse doesn't need. However, I am very good about getting my trailer checked once a year, on my birthday. That said, sometimes my trailer hero (aka mechanic) finds things that put me into sticker shock. If it's not critical, I make a mental note to make that repair "next time" or "next month." By the time I get home, my mind has already wandered off to the trail ride to which I was just invited. On this checklist, I have also added columns for the condition of the trailer and room for comments. With these added notes, you will remember what still needs repair, what % of usage you still have, and what your target repair date is. This is another list you should make copies of. I give one to the mechanic who repairs my trailer when I take it to him. When I pick the trailer up, we review it so he can tell me about necessary replacement of the floor boards that will cost $2,000. OUCH!! Since the floorboards are still at about 50%, we agree on a timeline of when they need to be replaced. I have my copy and he has his. I take my copy and make more - one gets taped to the inside of the tack room door so I look at it every time I grab my overpriced, unneeded bridle; one goes on my corkboard; and one goes in my calendar. You can even add an alert date on your phone, anything that will help you remember when you need the added service repair.

The bottom line is this- you don't need to replace everything at once, but you need to remember when you need to replace or repair it to keep your animals safe. If you get in the habit of tracking your repairs, you will find yourself worrying less because you won't be suffering equipment failure, even when you are trailering somewhere far and you have used your monthly allowance for fuel and more supplements that you don't need.

Trailer Maintenance Checklist

		Good	Fair	Needs work	Poor	Comments:
General:						
Over all condition:						
	Rust or decay					
	Damage to body of trailer					
Registration tags						
Coupler connection						
Safety chains						
Windows and drops						
Door access						
Latches						
Water tank						
Emergency Brake						
Hitch ball lubed						
Fire Extinguisher						
Road side equipment:						
	Flares					
	Triangles					
	Tire blocks					
	Trailer Jack					
Electrical						
Breaks						
Break away						
Turn Signal Lights						
Brake Lights						
Interior lights						
Additional exterior lights						
Electrical hitch						
Battery						
Reflectors						
Tires:						
Bearings						
Lug nuts						
Tread						
Wear						
Pressure						
Visible damage						
Spare condition						

Service Date:

	Follow up actions	Complete by	
1			
2			
3			
4			
5			
6			

The second part of keeping your trailer ready for emergencies is defining necessary contents of the trailer. If I go on an endurance ride or camping trip, I have 50 saddle bags, 30 containers of Coconut water, extras of this and that, and my gear. Since I am the clinic developer for large animal preparedness, I also have my trailer necessities. These are necessities that will stay in the trailer at all times. Many of the items on this list are things I use for my own personal situations as well as having them ready for emergencies and natural disasters.

Here is a true story that is an offshoot of this handbook but adds a bit of humor to a real injury. I was camping with my husband, Tom, near Paso Robles, CA. We had our two horses that we have had for some time and our new draft horse, Vievo, that we'd only about three months. They were in adjoining stalls, and as I cleaned one stall, I climbed between the panels into the next stall. I just assumed Vievo would act like the other two and not give a darn about my crawling through the panels behind him. I was so very wrong, as he did care. With one big kick from him I went flying backward into the rails. Once I realized nothing was broken and I could still walk, I limped back to camp only to find a big wet spot on my thigh where he had kicked me. Moments later (when I pulled my pants down in front of the public), I found my leg squirting subcutaneous fluid. He had split my leg open almost to the bone. We were not in any shape to drive to the hospital, and neither were our camping neighbors, so we had to make do with what we had. Fortunately, I kept our trailer packed for emergencies, so I was fully prepared and a little excited to use my emergency medical equipment. Since I was the injured one, Tom had to find all the medical material. It was easy because every clear container had a content list. We used the polo wraps, maxi pads, gauze, duct tape, and even a standing leg wrap to cover my leg. We had to re-wrap every 2 hours until the morning came when I could get to the emergency room. The moral of the story is multi-fold. One, being organized not only helps you during a natural disaster but it helps in any kind of emergency and results in less panic. Two, you will find that eventually you will need some of these supplies, if not for yourself then maybe for someone else. Three, one person in a group should always remain able to drive and take care of the horses.

When packing my trailer, I pack it in sections based on what I am most likely to use being the easiest to access and putting the least likely to use on the bottom or in back. Every trailer is different, so however you choose to store your supplies, you should organize by ease of access. Use clear plastic storage containers and label them with a general category, like "topical ointments" and a list of what is in each container. During my clinics, I ask a volunteer to find a band aid in an unorganized emergency container. After my timer has gone off, I send them to the trailer. The time it takes to find the container labeled "Human bandages and wraps" with a list that includes "Band-Aids" is less than half of what it takes to find it in the unorganized container. Clear labeling minimizes panic when searching for something in a limited amount of time.

Now I want to give you an idea of how our trailer is packed.

Here are some examples of how I pack my trailer:

Note: Gear Bag is easiest to access.

We also label our medicine cabinet.

Bottom row has containers we're least likely to use

This is a list of emergency equipment you should always keep in your trailer

Trailer Equipment List:

Horse:	People:
☐ 2-3 Halters	☐ Case of water
☐ Stud chain	☐ Flashlight with extra batteries
☐ Lunge Line	☐ Pillow case
☐ 3 Cotton Lead lines	☐ Book with map routes-can be in portfolio
☐ 3 large cotton, 1 Extra-large bandana	☐ Blanket
☐ Long Whip-Long enough to not get kicked	☐ Snacks
☐ Blanket	☐ 2 sets of gloves- work and warm
☐ 2 buckets-medium size	☐ 2 towels
☐ Cooking string	☐ Sunscreen
☐ Bailing twine	☐ Reflective Vest or reflectors that can be added to a top
☐ Filled water containers	☐ Bandanas (Grab Bag)
☐ Duct Tape (yes and extra roll)	
☐ Fly Mask	
☐ Towels 2/3	

☐ Emergency Medical Kit (s)

☐ Grab bag

☐ Portfolio Binder

☐ Trailer chocks

☐ Trailer Jack

☐ Extra Ropes

☐ Tool kit

☐ Road flares and/or safety triangles

☐ If possible, two-way radios

☐ Fire Extinguisher- visible & maintained

To make things a little easier, I follow a simple rule of thumb which is to replace at once after use. I note dates to replace oral and topical medicines on a calendar, and I always drain and refill my water tanks after I have used the trailer. If I have not used my trailer in a while, I drain and re-fill my water tanks every 3 months. The result of staying on top of the replacements is less panic when you need something during an emergency, because you have kept everything stocked and refilled. If you don't have a trailer but you have someone who will help you during an emergency, help them with the costs and preparation of the trailer. Also, buy them dinner!

Emergency Medical Kits

Use clear plastic containers and label with black Sharpie marker

Shared material

Bag 1- Wraps and Bandages
- ☐ Gauze wraps (sterile and non-sterile)
- ☐ Gauze pads (large and small)
- ☐ Q-tips
- ☐ Cotton Balls
- ☐ 2 rolls of self-adhesive vet wrap
- ☐ Adhesive Tape
- ☐ Scissors
- ☐ Small knife
- ☐ Safety pins
- ☐ 2 large tampons
- ☐ 2-3 large maxi pads
- ☐ Latex Gloves

Bag 2- Topicals
- ☐ Packaged Iodine swabs
- ☐ Neosporin Ointment
- ☐ Alcohol wipes
- ☐ Antibiotic Pouches
- ☐ Small sterile Eye wash

Misc Container
- ☐ Leg wraps
- ☐ Duct tape
- ☐ Flashlight/batteries
- ☐ Small & large knife
- ☐ Large Bandana
- ☐ Rope
- ☐ Extra vet wraps
- ☐ 6 gallon size plastic bags/ 4 kitchen-sized trash bags

Horse container: Emergency Material for horses only
- ☐ Banamine Paste
- ☐ Bute Paste
- ☐ Ace
- ☐ Hoof boot
- ☐ Hoof pick
- ☐ Small dose of horse prescriptions

People container:
- ☐ Aspirin
- ☐ Tylenol
- ☐ band aids (different sizes)
- ☐ Burn dressing & cream
- ☐ Benadryl
- ☐ Auto-activated Cold Pack
- ☐ Tweezers
- ☐ Hand sanitizer
- ☐ Mask
- ☐ Gorilla Glue
- ☐ Blood stopper (anti-coagulant)

Replace topicals and oral meds every 6 months | Sterile Material: replace once a year

The Grab bag is the most important item of your emergency equipment. It should be the easiest item to access whether it is in your trailer, home or truck/car. You will need this before you evacuate. Keep this checklist in the bag and use a thick Sharpie marker to clearly identify it as Grab Bag.

Grab Bag: separating items into plastic bags keeps small items together

- ☐ Two Bottles of water, in doubled plastic bags
- ☐ Set of safety goggles
- ☐ 4 sets of Latex Gloves (in sandwich bag)
- ☐ Small roll of duct tape
- ☐ Pen bag - Use a sandwich bag
  - 2 Med Sharpie Markers (one red)
  - 1 Thick Sharpie Marker
  - 2 Regular writing pens
- ☐ Notebook in plastic bag
- ☐ 2 Bandanas
- ☐ Extra Batteries (sized for the flashlights)
- ☐ Head lamp
- ☐ Regular Flashlight (one that can stand alone)
- ☐ Gloves (in sandwich bag)
- ☐ All equine identification: Bands, dog tags, reflective tape, etc. (in plastic bag)
- ☐ Small dose (2-3 days) of personal prescription medicines (in plastic bag)
- ☐ Leatherman knife, straight knife, scissor
- ☐ Facemasks
- ☐ Hat
- ☐ 2 Extra Cell phone chargers, in plastic bag

Go Bag:

1. If you partner with anyone, double the above equipment to allow for sharing
2. Grab bag checkup- 2 times per year with a reminder on your calendar

There is nothing worse than reaching for your grab bag and finding a wet, smelly jungle of mold. I also sub-bag my batteries with my flashlights.

The next item of importance is the ownership portfolio. This is a simple binder that keeps all important records regarding your horse. You CAN NEVER over identify. This portfolio is not only a useful tool for emergencies, but it is also very helpful when traveling out of state or to public events. You only need one 3 ring binder for all your animals; just separate the animals by tabs. We have two horses, one tab for each. Keep the portfolio in your trailer or very close to your grab bag. If you don't have a trailer, grab your portfolio when you grab your grab bag. The portfolio should be an 8x11 binder, so you don't confuse it with your adult novel.

Ownership Portfolio: Standard Binder with tabs

Section 1-

- ☐ Stall Hangers with Twine already attached (each horse)

Section 2-

- ☐ Copy of registration (each horse)
- ☐ 2-3 images of different angles of horse with owner in picture (each horse)
- ☐ Emergency Contact list
- ☐ Evacuation Plan and Map Routes
- ☐ Neighborhood Planning Sheet
- ☐ List of social media sites and phone apps that put you in communication with highway conditions, emergency status, evacuation sites and available resources

Section 3-

- ☐ Emergency Contact Information, with Authorization for handling 2-3 copies
- ☐ Vet records - updated
- ☐ Coggins (if available, can be old)
- ☐ Health Certificate (if available, can be old)
- ☐ ID images that may connect you to your horse
- ☐ Photos of animal's Chestnuts, Whorls, freeze brands, other ID

For quick access, it is best to put your Emergency Contact list in the front.

As part of this portfolio, I include Stall Hangers. These are effective ways to make sure your large animal is properly identified while at an evacuation site. They can be hung with twine or duct taped on the stall or pen. I also use these when we are camping or at an event. It even works for Brahma bulls. Here is an example of a stall hanger:

Stall Hangers: to hang on stalls or corrals at remote camping, ranch or Evacuation sites

IMAGE: (you with your horse)

Name:
Breed/Sex/Color:

Owner:
Primary #:   Secondary #:
Emergency Contact:
Relationship:
Telephone #:
Diet Restriction: You do not want volunteers feeding your animal something would be bad for him. "WARNING" - very important if your animal can be dangerous. Example, is your Brahma bull safe to lead around the fairgrounds?

- Make 3 copies- approximately 8x11 standard size with information on both sides
- Laminate
- 3-hole punch to hang from stall with twine or other material
- Example:

Name: Om El Love Him
Arabian Gelding: Grey
Owner: V. We really love him
Emergency Telephone #: 888-888-0000
Secondary Contact: Oh My Hubby
Emergency Contact: 999-999-0000
Diet Restriction: None
Warning: Doesn't like kids with hats

There is some debate about the stall hangers. I choose to laminate so it is weather proof, will not slip out of the pocket and is harder for the animal to eat.

The final bag to keep in your trailer is your clothing bag. Pick a bag you rarely use and label it as Extra Clothing.

Clothing Bag:

☐ Jacket – Medium and raincoat

☐ Underwear (in plastic bag)

☐ Two pairs of socks

☐ Warm hat, regular hat & extra gloves

☐ T-shirt, Sweatshirt, Sweatpants

☐ Extra pants

☐ Shoes

☐ Beach towel

☐ Toilet paper (in a bag)

Optional:

Toiletry bag with toothpaste, toothbrush, small dose of meds, hair bands, etc.
I don't think this list needs a lot of explanation, except the toilet paper and underwear in a bag.
If you don't understand these two, please ask your best friend or beer drinking buddy.

It doesn't help if your animal is not prepared...

Come on boy - we gotta go!

The first step to planning is to train yourself. I know there is an emphasis on training your animals, but you cannot train your animals unless you first train yourself. Part of this is to make sure the prior preparation steps are completed. Training yourself is so important because it helps to prepare you for the guaranteed chaos when an emergency occurs. There will be panic for sure. It could be you panicking or others around you. Remember the story I told you about my getting kicked in the leg? The moment my husband realized that it wasn't the horse's urine on my leg and it was subcutaneous fluid coming from my open leg wound, he panicked. Fortunately, I've trained myself to be prepared and stay calm. I did not need to spend a lot of time explaining where the emergency items were because everything was clearly marked. He was only mildly panicked because I was screaming my head off.

Train yourself to check your emergency essentials, to keep up with repairs, to note oral and topical expirations, to replace your water storage, and to update your emergency contact list. This is a reason to have another fun BBQ in 3 months. Also, keep up with your portfolio to include updating pictures as you and your animals get older (I know we never age), replace your emergency contact list as it changes, and update vet records and your personal information. When the emergency occurs, you will find yourself less panicked because you have properly planned and properly trained yourself for an emergency. By being well trained, you will be able to properly assess the situation around you and help your friends, because they may be running around like chickens with their heads cut off. That is, unless you have bought them a copy of this handbook and they have trained themselves as well.

Another important step to training yourself is to learn how to stay calm in an emergency. To do this, you must put yourself in situations that may make you uncomfortable. If you are uncomfortable speaking publicly, then come with me to one of my clinics and I will train you right away. If you are uncomfortable around people who have no control, put on a pair of roller skates and hit the roller rink. Do you get the point? Plain and simple, train yourself to control your panic. Proper planning and proper training will help reduce your panic, help you communicate (there's that word again) with others and your animals, help you keep calm, and then you'll remember that you are already prepared. Once you train yourself for these types of emergencies, you will find that you can handle yourself much differently in your personal life. That will be an extra $200 for this therapy session!

OK, now that you are calm, cool and collected, you are ready to take on the world and any emergency that does arise. You're prepared to get your Brahma bull to safety without panicking. However, have you fully prepared him for emergencies, including the natural disasters? It would be extremely difficult to convince the big guy to load if you have not properly trained him.

Training your livestock to cooperate during an emergency is quite different than standard training techniques. As a former horse trainer, I look at myself now and cringe at what I am saying. When I present clinics, I see the trainers pucker their lips and scowl at me while I talk about doing things that are completely contrary to other ways of training large animals. The problem is that things change dramatically and quickly in an emergency. In a normal, calm situation, one can quietly direct their animal and drive him into a trailer. Whether it be yours or someone else's trailer, you have the time to spend and create the perfect environment. During an emergency, you are moving fast and the people around you are moving fast. Equally important is that your animal needs to move fast for you and him to escape danger. Add the smell of fire, mud coming at full speed, or water rising around them and you, and the circumstances change even faster.

The first step in training your large animal is to teach them how to handle panic. This is where the trainers scowl at me. During my clinic, part of my presentation is called, "Musical Horse." I will walk calmly with the horse in tow, usually an unknown horse, and suddenly start singing and dancing to "Staying Alive." There are a few outcomes to this unorthodox method - 1) the horse freaks out at the sudden movement and tries to escape because we've just gone from calmness to pretend panic 2) the horse hates my singing and the owner complains or 3) I adjust my level of energy, so he can slowly adapt to my sudden changes in behavior. At a recent clinic, I was working with a very cute little filly. Her escape mode was to rear and turn away, thus resulting in me with no horse attached. I restarted at a much lower energy level, slowly working her up to the sudden changes that she could experience with a person who was in panic mode. I did have to use some of my old traditional training methods to overcome the bolting and rearing. However, in the end, the mare was able to sing "Staying Alive" right along with me and she held a better note. Transition up and get the animals to handle your level of energy changes. Practice leading them calmly and suddenly acting crazy and panicked. If need be, drink some of that energy drink or a shot of Tequila before you practice. The goal of the training is learning how to *communicate* with your animal and to have your animal look at you and say, "No problem, I can handle whatever you're going to give".

This cute little horse originally had a bit of a meltdown but was soon very tired of my antics and began singing along with me. Photo credit to Dale Lofgren.

The second step to training your animal is to teach him how to be handled by other people and even panicked people. You may be calm, cool and collected while leading your trained animal to the trailer, but suddenly you realize you have forgotten that bag of $300 custom blend pellets. Urgently, you look for someone who can hold your animal while you frantically run off to grab your pellets. How does your animal respond to someone unknown that comes with a different type of panicked energy? You can help your animal learn how to deal with this by practicing the scenario, "Duck, Duck, Horse." This can make for a fun day, and, of course, a BBQ. Thanks to high demand, this part of training has become a very popular clinic in itself. Guess why it is called, "Duck, Duck, Horse". You will want at least 5 animals and 7-9 people. Do not get more than 10 animals, as it makes for too much chaos. I would not suggest doing this with cattle; maybe camels are ok, but not cattle. If you are practicing with goats, you can have about 15 - 20. All animals should be in a fenced arena and lined up. The object is to rotate animal handlers at different levels of energy. I use fun, high energy music. The goal for the animals is to calmly adapt to the constantly changing people and high energy of the arena environment. In my last clinic, I had 3 volunteers pretend to play football. I do not make this a normal part of my clinics, but everyone felt that it was a lot of fun.

Finally, there is trailer training. While I love to add a splash of humor, this is serious and could cost your animals their lives. A general rule of thumb for many evacuation volunteers is to allow about 5-10 minutes to load the animal. Let's give you an example to show the level of importance for this process. The fire races down the hill towards your animals and you have 2 horses and 1 Alpaca. In normal circumstances, they load and trailer together very well. But now there is fire and panic. The two horses are in the trailer, but you cannot get your Alpaca to load. The fire is dangerously close, and you are forced to make the decision to leave him behind. Will there be tears? Now you may understand why it is important to teach them to load in different types of trailers, with different levels of energy by different people. It seems like a chore, and I know you will procrastinate because it just doesn't sound like fun; but, it can be fun and effective at the same time. This is the perfect setting for another social, fun filled, great food event where people get together. Ideally, you will want to have a slant load, a straight load, a step up and a ramp choice of trailers. You can use the same technique as the "Duck, Duck, Horse" to change out people when loading. It is important to remember that the horses can do this for only so long. It will take a lot of mental energy, so patience and time are mandatory. If you have a big group, I highly recommend you hire a professional trainer that can help you and the animals. If you are a group of private residents, you can always hold an event at someone's property, or you can find a shared or common arena.

As you now realize, training yourself may be an important part of the equation but training your animal is equally important. Your ability to stay calm will communicate that everything is going to be okay. And the calmness in your animal will communicate that they trust you and will cooperate with your unnatural behavior.

Preparation + Communication with others and your animals + training yourself= **Planning**

Proper planning + training **= Calmness**

Chapter II

Prepare......

Defining the Intent of Prepare

"Prepare" is a word often confused with "Plan". How often do we prepare our meals, our guest list for the *summer* party, or to get ready for an emergency evacuation?

According to this picture, is this too late to prepare?

Photo credit to Kimberly Rivers.
Picture is blurry because it's an actual scene during the Thomas Fire 2017

The fastest moving fire in California, the Thomas Fire, emphasized how important it is to understand the meaning of "prepare" before an emergency. This is one of the most confusing words to large animal owners. To prepare is not to plan - it is to get ready to leave, to go. A well-known phrase is *"ready, set, go"*. Prepare is the *"set"* part of this saying. By preparing in advance, you will be ready to go. Because you have taken the time to plan, you are 3/4 prepared - packed, trained and calm.

Taking the Steps to Prepare

Preparing is knowing when it is time to get packed, confirm details and have your animal's identification on each of them. Since you have done all of your planning homework, there are only a few additional steps needed to prepare. The first step is paying attention to when it is time to prepare. We all say it - "oh, that won't happen to me," or "I didn't know it was happening so fast," or "I thought I would have more time." The time to prepare is the minute you see or hear the warning. It is very important to remember the saying we hear the fire department, local sheriff and CHP say, *Don't wait until it's too late.* Your warning signs are your weather alerts and news reports. High winds, red flag & flood advisories, thunderstorms, tornado warnings, and excessive rain are all "red alert" words which you must listen for and be alert to responding. The weather "people" may not always be on the nose, but if they are correct, then you are prepared; and if they are not right, you were able to practice preparing. Think of it as a good cook would (okay, if you're not a cook, ask a friend who is); it is far better to have too much food than not enough.

Start preparing the minute you hear any disturbing weather warnings. You do not have to act, but just be ready. Start with getting your gear together and preparing your vehicles.

- ☐ Fill up your truck and check all fluid levels.

- ☐ If possible, hook up your trailer - or at least set it up for easy connection and parked in the exit direction.

- ☐ Check your water tanks.

- ☐ Put 2-3 days of feed plus any supplements in your vehicle or trailer.

- ☐ Make sure your spare keys are in the correct location.

- ☐ Check your fire extinguisher and put an extra in your vehicle.

- ☐ Contact your emergency contacts to confirm plans and emergency meeting areas.

- ☐ Put an extra phone charger in your vehicle.

- ☐ For those who will be relying on someone else to trailer, make contact and confirm the plans. Offer to help prepare. And, buy them dinner.

- ☐ Pack snacks ready for your vehicle.

- ☐ If available, charge your sets of 2-way radios and put them in your vehicle.

- ☐ Put a headlamp with fresh batteries in your vehicle.

- ☐ Program emergency contact applications in your phone. Update your social media direct contact list to agency links to avoid the "social media chaos".

☐ If possible, shelter some of your feed some place off your property to protect it from being lost but have it available should the feed area on your property get damaged. Since you are preparing in advance, without being rushed or panicked, you may even have time to scrub the mats in the trailer, mix yourself a drink and watch a little bit of that movie, Twister!

Now it's time to get your animals prepped. It will not take much time since you already spent a lot of time training them; but it is important to remember to prepare your animals for "go time."

☐ Put your identification on your animals: Brightly colored fetlock bands with telephone numbers sewn in (you can purchase these from on-line stores like EquestriSafe), bright dog tags braided into the horse's mane and tail with shoe laces or bright string. All of this should be together in your grab bag.

At least 3 dog tags in mane-seriously-hang them below the end of the mane

Fetlock bands

☐ Put brightly colored dog tags on halters.

☐ Move animals to an area that is easy access and where it is easy to catch them.

☐ Hang halters and <u>cotton</u> lead lines on fences so they are easy to put on the correct animals.

☐ Start feeding electrolytes. If the animals are evacuated to a remote site, the stress of the new environment and change in water flavor may affect the animal's health. Feeding electrolytes will help to make sure your animal is well hydrated should you have to evacuate. Additionally, flavored electrolytes can be used to help mask unfamiliar water.

☐ Take shavings and bedding out of stalls.

☐ Take off all blankets and halters.

- [ ] If possible, start moving animals to a friend's place that would be out of the danger zone.

There are several theories about how to identify your animals and what to use. I minimize the identification needs because I focus on advanced planning and preparation needs. Some believe you should only use a leather halter because nylon melts. That is a correct statement, but if you are properly prepared to evacuate, the type of halter should not matter because you will not be that close to the danger. Others recommend writing your telephone number on the animal's foot. Have you ever tried this? Since you spent so much time planning and training, your animals are now bomb proof and show utter calmness, but you will still have a hard time writing on their foot. Try it but have the emergency kit ready. In part of my clinic, I have volunteers come up with a Sharpie marker, and I give them the choice to write on my foot or my horse's foot. The outcome is the same because it is very difficult to write anywhere if you have an animal or person that is moving around. The few that tried to write on my foot tried to use some inappropriate places to hold on to me, and it made for some good laughs. My horse and I usually finish the clinic without any writing on our feet. Duct tape is another common idea, but it can come off. Pull it, apply it, and write your telephone number. Again, I hope you do not need it because you were properly prepared. Also, pulling and tearing duct tape next to an animal's rear end is something you may want to practice wearing a chest protector. Finally, there are suggestions to use a Sharpie marker to write directly on the animal. If the animal is light colored, it may be ok. If the animal is dark colored, it may be difficult to write on them using a White Out marker. A cattle marker will write easily on a horse, so buy one beforehand and mark the rump.

The important factor in preparing for you and your animals is to be ready to go with minimal panic and plenty of time BEFORE you are in harm's way. Knowing you have already taken steps to prepare will be of great comfort to you by relieving a lot of stress.

Chapter III

Implement......

Go Time

What is go time? For many people, this means when the emergency is upon them. Sometimes we confuse "go time" even in personal emergencies. When your animal is down, groaning, and hasn't eaten for two days, "go time" to call out a veterinarian is probably a day too late. In the case of a fire, "go time" for most is once they hear the fire is already close to their property. In the case of mudslides, it's usually not until they hear the sound of the slide. For flooding, it's not until the waters have started rising around you. The commonality to all of these "go times" is that the outcome can be tragic and it may be too late to do anything.

Burnt hills at our ranch in Santa Paula. It took less than two hours to reach and burn

Load your animals in order of dependency. What? No, they don't have drug or alcohol dependencies, but they may have buddy dependencies. Load the more independent animal first and the others will follow, just like "Follow the Leader." Even with all the practice, the actual emergency will send a charge through the air and the animals will feel it. Yes, they will be much calmer because you took the time to train and plan, but they may still be somewhat anxious. The more dependent animals will rely on the stronger independent animals as their leaders. Load the independent ones first and the others will follow.

No, not the blankets! Don't blanket or put fly masks on your animals even though your partner is telling you it will protect their eyes. Well, okay, put the fly masks on after you are out of danger. Don't forget to write your name and number on the masks because they will most definitely disappear at an evacuation site. There is a myth that putting blankets and fly masks on will protect the animals. It is not true, and, actually, it will interfere far more than help. Such gear could become dangerous while evacuating and even while in a trailer; and, if evacuated to a site that has only stalls with unknown animals next to yours, the fly masks could prevent your horse from seeing quickly and easily or even get caught on something. The blankets can slip even in the trailer and will easily get lost at an evacuation site.

Get on the road early, especially if you are going to make multiple trips. It is important to remember that you will not be the only one desperately trying to escape the area. The longer you wait, the worse the traffic will be. For people with livestock, it is even more difficult because we cannot maneuver vehicles as well. The minute the weather changes, it is time for you to go. Do not wait until the mudslide is coming down the mountain, the waters have reached your gate, or the fire is behind your property. That is way too late. Another important consideration is keeping access open for the emergency departments to mitigate the emergency. By waiting until it is too late to go, you are putting your animals in danger and becoming part of a problem. Even if the evacuation sites are not open yet, you have already set up a safe meeting place so you can wait there until the danger has passed or the evacuation sites have opened. It is better to be prepared and leave early than leave too late. You can always go back once you know it is safe.

Your Animals and the Evacuation Facility

Not only is an evacuation stressful for you and your animals, but the evacuation sites will be just as stressful, possibly more so, because of the chaos and panic going on around you. Of course, many of those people didn't attend one of my clinics or read the book so they and their animals are literally freaking out. Not you or your animals - all are calm, cool and collected. Even though you have planned and prepared, there will still be some stress, but it will certainly be much less. Now, it's time to settle your animals to be as comfortable as possible while at the evacuation site.

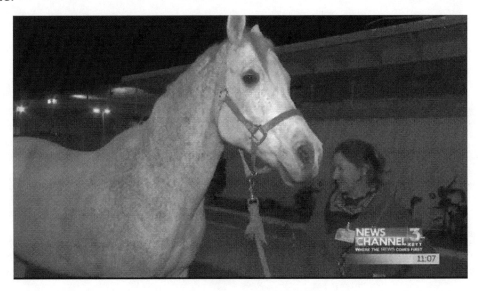

Photo credit: Keyt 3 News. My horse, Om El Salaam, was irritated by the upset animals

The dependent and independent animals will rely on each other so keep the process the same. Remember when we discussed loading in order of the independent animal followed by dependent animals? The same will apply once you arrive. At my clinics I have been asked about unloading, so I will touch on the unloading process. The question presented to me on more than one occasion is, "Do we unload our animals in the same order we loaded them?" Take a moment to think about this. Goats, llamas, pigs, and other smaller animals may move during the trailer ride. The minute you step in the trailer at the evacuation area, they will realize they are at a new place full of strange people that are freaking out, and they will make it difficult for you to catch them. My recommendation is to catch what you can and hold them just outside the trailer so the others are easier to catch. Important reminder for these smaller livestock animals - they move fast so get in and out of your trailer as quickly as possible, with someone closing the door behind you. As far as larger animals, unless there is some magic, they are usually in the same spot as you loaded them. Believe it or not, the unloading process should not be that difficult. When loading the animals into the trailer, you used the most independent animal to coax the others to follow. When unloading the animals, the dependent animals are now being taken away from their leader, so they will unload easier and wait for the herd leader to rejoin them. When unloading any animal at an evacuation site, remember to keep the animals as close to the trailer as possible until all animals are out of it. This will minimize stress and separation anxiety.

Housing the animals also requires some quick action. Once at the facility, you will not have a lot of control of who goes where, but there is a high chance you will be able to house the animals close to each other. If they are in open stalls, it will be easier on them since they will be able to see each other and interact. If they are in box stalls, it may be a bit more stressful. Either way, you will want to continue practicing the dependent and independent theory; when leading two or more animals, it is easier for the dependent animal to walk away versus first leading the independent animal away. That is the same order you will use to stable the animals. Put the independent animal in the first stall and take the dependent animal(s) to the other assigned stall(s). With multiple animals ask if some can be housed together. If they cannot, the most dependent animal should be the last to put in a stall/box stall. A perfect example of this theory is from the recent Thomas Fire. We had to put a mare and her colt in a barn. The owners wanted them separate, so we found two box stalls that were together. Two members of my team put the colt in the box stall first. He was okay until they started to lead his mom away. He panicked, jumped the door and landed on two of the volunteers. We got him to safety and put his mom in the stall while he watched. After letting them nose for just a bit, we led him to the stall next door. She was not the one leaving him, so he was more confident and he knew where she was. He was still upset but much more manageable. Moral of the story - let the dependent animals see where the leader is and walk them away, not vice versa.

However, you check in and set up the animals is important because you are setting the animals up for the safest and most comfortable situation possible and thus minimizing their stress. There are different processes for animal intake, but there should always be someone taking information about the animals and owners when you arrive. They are usually the ones who assign the stalls. If the form does not already have it, make sure you provide two (2) back up emergency contacts (if possible, give then a copy of your emergency contact form), notate if you or someone else will be feeding the animals, what they will be fed and any allergies and medical conditions. You probably already have this in your portfolio but make sure something is attached to the official intake form. Once you are checked in and have confirmed that all information has been provided to the intake crew, it is time to get your animals settled.

- ☐ Put your Stall Hanger up. If your animals are in a pen, you can use the twine to secure them. If they are in box stalls, use duct tape. On rare occasions animals will be held in an arena and tied to the sides. If this is the case, you can still attach the stall hanger in front of where they are tied. If your animal chews, double secure it. The lamination makes it harder for the animals to destroy it if they do chew.

- ☐ Keep all the identification on the animals in case they get loose. The brightness of the dog tags and fetlock bands will make it easy for the volunteers and staff to contact you should something happen. I use a neon breakaway collar that has my name and contact information in a card holder on the collar.

- ☐ You should set up the animal's water. Remember when you started giving electrolytes during your preparation? Put some in the water, especially if flavored. If you can, use a bucket they are already familiar with from home.

- ☐ If possible, make them a bran mash of some sort. What's your comfort food? Mine is chocolate, so if I must be evacuated to a box stall, my husband has been given the directive to bring me lots of chocolate. Having a mash not only guarantees moisture in the gut but it helps calm them down.

☐ Take off the halters. I know there's a lot of different opinions about this, but remember, animals get in trouble. Even though their holding area looks safe, they will still find something and some way to get entangled. If you feel you need to keep something on them, use a break away halter, and just make this part of your trailer equipment.

☐ Set up a feeding log, and you can add this to your portfolio ahead of time. Basically, it tracks the date and has check boxes for am and pm feedings. Every time you feed, check it off. If you have someone helping to feed, ask that person to check it off as well. This way you will always know if a meal was missed.

☐ Finally, put yourself back into your calm state and reassure yourself and your horses - remember the communication training and that they rely on you now.

So, your animals are settled, you have calmed down a bit, you have parked your trailer, and you are just anxiously waiting to find out if your property is safe. While you are there, remember to thank the volunteers and staff at the evacuation sites. Do what you can to help them. It can be from managing and cleaning your own animal's stall to helping them with the other animals by checking water and keeping an eye out for odd behavior. Your help will make a difference to them, and you will be active around the grounds, learning the behavior of your animals around the others. If you are feeling exceptionally appreciative, go buy them coffee, donuts, cookies and burritos. When you are ready to take your animals home, try to clean up to the best of your ability. It will make it a lot easier for the staff and volunteers.

Chapter IV

Finding Outside Help

Despite all your planning and consistent communication, you still may need help evacuating your animals. Most people have heard the horror stories of a nice, unknown volunteer offering to help evacuate your animals only to have them disappear. Or, while in tow, something happens to the animal. If you do need to call for help, I recommend the following:

☐ Remember when you programmed the important agency information on your phone? One of those numbers should be the emergency contact for Animal Services Evacuation Assistance. Call them first, before posting any requests for help on random social media sites. Animal services usually has staff and/or assigned volunteer groups that can aid with evacuating your animal. They are working under agency directive.

☐ Make sure to give your dispatch contact as much information as possible, including a meeting destination, especially if you have to get your animals to a safe location close enough for you to walk them. Ask what agency is coming (Animal Services, Posse, certified evacuation teams) so you can watch for them and wave them down if you are not on your property or on the property of the boarding facility.

☐ Have your animals out of the stalls, in front of your property and ready to load. If you are at a boarding facility, have them in the parking area closest to the entrance and exit. Remember, time is of the essence for you and everyone else in the danger zone.

☐ Give the rescuer a copy of your Emergency Contact Form. If you are separated for any reason, or you cannot make it to the evacuation site right away, that paperwork will help get the animals checked and ensure all important data has been recorded so they know how to contact you. When you do arrive, it will be easier for the volunteers to identify you since they have already been given your information. Use your Portfolio to document ownership.

☐ If it can be avoided, do not reach out via social media groups unless you absolutely must. While good Samaritan volunteers usually have good intentions, there are still risks - they do not know where to go, they may be unfamiliar with the area and get lost, they are probably not properly insured to protect themselves or your animals if they are injured, and by not acting as part of the agency coordinated effort they may become part of the problem. In some cases, some volunteers do not have good intentions at all, and they are there to steal your animals, which is easy to do when owners are under duress. If you absolutely must reach out in this manner, here are some suggestions:

  o Take a picture of both vehicles, showing the trailer license plate and towing vehicle license plate. The pictures should also show the make and model of both vehicles.

  o Give the transporter a paper with your telephone number and name and also the name and address of the location to where the animals should be transported. You can write this out while you wait for help to arrive.

  o Take a picture of their driver's license.

o   Get the driver's full name and cell number. While you are standing there, make a quick call to confirm the number is correct.

o   Have the driver repeat your name and the location to where the animals are being transported.

Conclusion

As you finish this handbook, you are probably thinking, "Are you kidding, this is way too much work!" I must agree, and it does sound like a lot to put together and coordinate. Some people mistakenly think everything must be done at once. Many people walk away from my clinics very motivated, but lack follow through (which is why this book was written). Many people leave my clinics motivated and follow through with immediate plans to implement. Some have even sent me their calendars to show how they have set up their trainings. It is always fun to get invited back to watch a prior clinic's group training session or to hold one of my additional "fun" clinics. It really sounds like it is more work than it is. Remember that you have spent money and time on your animals, and they are worth doing everything you can to make sure they are safe during emergencies. If nothing else works, use this handbook as a reason to schedule some get togethers and BBQ's. Good food, good drinks and good laughs make it easier to plan, train and prepare. It is not unusual to have a lot of laughter during your trainings. After all, how many people really can dance to the song, "Staying Alive," while trying to walk with their animals? The more fun you make it, the better you will be prepared, and you will always keep the lines of communication open for when the emergencies do occur.

By setting up your trailer equipment, you will not only be prepared for the emergency, but you will always be up to date on your medicines. You can set it up in increments, so everything doesn't have to be done at once. Make a deal with yourself like I do. I calendar the days I need to replace my oral and topical trailer supplies. My reward is 3 scoops of my favorite ice cream. Yes, I did say three, and I can eat it all. Keeping up with your trailer maintenance is something every large animal owner should do, even when they are not in a danger zone. Remember, the trailer is your animal's palace. They make the choice to trust you every time they step in it.

The bottom line is that your communication skills are tested from the beginning to the end of an emergency. You improve communication with your neighbors and friends while you plan; you improve communication with your animals while you train; and you use those calming communication skills to get your animals to safety. You will also use those skills to communicate with staff at the evacuation sites.

Use this handbook as a tool to prepare, not only for natural disasters, but for emergencies that may occur while at a show, at the fair, driving the highways, or on a camping trip.

I hope you will find this handbook to be very helpful. After reading it, you may be interested in sponsoring a PPI clinic. By filling a day with laughter and learning important knowledge that will protect you and your animals during emergencies – that is success. Please feel free to contact me, and I will be glad to further discuss the clinics. Remember to have some laughs during your preparation and planning as a sense of humor will help you survive all emergencies in life.

Made in United States
Troutdale, OR
09/22/2024

23046488R10029